DIGITAL DETOX

DIGITAL DETOX

GIDEON RAYBURN

CONTENTS

1	Introduction	1
2	Chapter 1: Understanding Digital Dependency	3
3	Chapter 2: Benefits of Digital Detox	7
4	Chapter 3: Strategies for a Successful Digital Det	11
5	Chapter 4: Mindfulness in the Digital Age	15
6	Chapter 5: Creating a Digital Detox Plan	19
7	Chapter 6: Overcoming Challenges	23
8	Chapter 7: Maintaining a Balanced Digital Lifestyl	25
9	Chapter 8: Impact of Digital Detox on Relationship	27
10	Chapter 9: Digital Detox and Physical Health	29
11	Chapter 10: Raising Digital Detox Kids	33
12	Chapter 11: Digital Detox and Personal Growth	37
13	Chapter 12: Digital Detox and Professional Develop	41
14	Chapter 13: Social Media and Self-Esteem	45
15	Chapter 14: The Future of Digital Detox	49
16	Conclusion	53
17	References	55

Copyright © 2024 by Gideon Rayburn
All rights reserved. No part of this book may be reproduced in any manner whatsoever without written permission except in the case of brief quotations embodied in critical articles and reviews.
First Printing, 2024

CHAPTER 1

Introduction

There are some important caveats. The most important is not to expect a lifetime solution. By taking a very deliberate break, it is possible to adopt healthy new patterns and habits, and life afterwards may be lived in a sensible way. But most of us have to learn the hard way that old habits are not so easily broken. And unless your friends and family have also had a digital detox, they might be grumpy with you the whole way through. The authors are aware that their lives depend heavily on these platforms, that to a large extent their networks are their work, and that they will be required to return to them. Relinquishing digital tools and spaces permanently is simply not an option. The suggestion that workplaces should tolerate digital detoxes is ridiculous.

What we believe is that with digital detoxes, we can return to our publics with our own understandings of these platforms and spaces, our use and absorption of them no longer determined by a consensus around the value and utility of engaging online, reinforced by accounts of what others are up to and the daily compulsion of social media. The alternative—never leaving these spaces—is not neutral. Remaining deeply enmeshed in an increasingly one-dimensional public environment may have a profound effect on world views, values, and practices. The detox is worth it, even if others do not join us.

CHAPTER 2

Chapter 1: Understanding Digital Dependency

I always imagined I would unplug so often from the digital world. In fact, I had no intention of being this hooked on digital life - I hadn't even set my mind to such a thought several years ago when I received my first email account at the age of eighteen. I remember hanging out in the messaging system with the others, talking until the wee hours about anything and everything imaginable. With it, family members I haven't seen in a long time would come in contact with me, researchers would invite me to present my papers at conferences, and I was to keep in touch with my new faculty and academic contacts there. Little did I know that it was only the beginning.

Bear in mind that all of these social networking platforms people currently have were not known to us at the time. The biggest thing that could happen to a communication and connection loving girl was AOL, the worldwide web, ICQ, and the possibility to call people in peak paying just for the internet fee that was dialing my connections when outside peak hours.

The Impact of Technology on Society

Digital Detox: Reclaiming Your Life in a Hyperconnected World, by Damon Zahariades

Over the past thirty years, the world of the twenty-first century has come into existence, characterized by the transformation from a system based on industry into another based on new technologies to an ever greater extent. It is true that the impact of technology is not always positive, and that swift, blindly said impact may even bring about harmful results to society if it is not appropriately handled. It is probably not excessive to claim that the computer has changed the very life of society in the space of the same number of years in which farming methods or the highway system did so in the space of 3000 years.

Before addressing the impact of technology on society, it may be worthwhile to point out briefly what technology is, as well as what it is not. The concept "technology" was traditionally used to refer to that branch of knowledge which deals with the creation of tools. According to this traditional way of thinking, technology is a normative discipline oriented towards the design of desirable and beneficial artifacts. The so-called ethical hacking is often conceived because of the commitment to assuring the ownership of the knowledge tools, versus an exclusion of some groups of people, or from the wish of safeguarding the integrity of the critical infrastructures.

However, technology also respects a more fundamental circularity as this, an inescapable circularity. Thanks to the advancement of technology, so many benefits are experienced both by the individual and by the people interdependently, that technology could not result in life without moral principles. Technology, in the course of time, has assumed authority in the current focused on aspects of people's lives and of society in general. The debate is extremely heated around the implicit ethical abdications on which the enhancement of technology is based is that the fact of being also occupied in the penetration of the behavioral patterns adopted in many instances, only as regards the many changes that, in humans and in their interaction, occur in particular, or in limited sectors such as health care.

Technology itself, according to the most unrecognized part of its purpose, attributes goals that concern it. Technology is originated by an individual, but cannot be considered as separate from the fact that it involves subjects physically, that it designs things and that it will be designed by others. The history of the individual and that of technology are closely related; it is not possible to separate them from one another. The people, moreover, are engaged in a need for knowledge in relation to the imposition of the entire cultural epistemic base of which economics provides the foundation, economics that studies the production and the distribution of the economic goods.

In conclusion, the individual dimensions and the collective models develop in parallel, determining the knowledge of fine linkages and oppositions.

Signs of Digital Addiction

Scientists propose a two-week plan and then another 48-week approach to kick addiction. First, reduce media connections: work while disconnected, arrange technological blackout times (like skipping an evening movie), and cut back gradually. Regularly turn off your e-mail and your smartphone. Next, poster your way to transition by displaying visual reminders like good old-fashioned glued-on sticky notes to help you maintain a goal. If absolute abstinence feels too daunting, tell someone about the benefits of reducing communication channels. Privacy is not a given, so beware of snoopers. Indeed, broadcast (trounce) your technology-free time by adding a white-noise download to drown out your keystrokes and other activity. Also, tell someone. In the initial phase of staying offline, encounter the real world with other people. Encourage others to join you in tech-free time. Then, take another step toward freedom with a week of continued disconnection - without back-to-reality reminders of what you have been missing. Resist the temptation to return to digital life. This later phase hinges on whether you can rally control when making technological choices.

When it comes to technology addiction, the Diagnostic and Statistical Manual of Mental Disorders (DSM), considered the "bible of psychiatry," has yet to formally recognize it as an illness. All the same, the DSM considers internet use to be compulsive, and most mental health professionals view spending too many hours online as a symptom of existing disorders like anxiety and depression. Like these pathologies, compulsive internet use can result in negative life consequences. These can include marital problems, financial troubles, job loss, and carpal tunnel as well as neck and back pain - all from hours spent hunched over a computer. Other potential risks should not be overlooked. Over time, excessive technology use can actually alter the brain - it's not just an addiction issue. The prefrontal cortex, the seat of impulse control, can become suppressed after exposure to social media.

CHAPTER 3

Chapter 2: Benefits of Digital Detox

While people understand the consequences technology has on damaging their focus, it is good to know that there are simple solutions: disconnect from the world through what is known as digital detox. The goal of this process is to help individuals reduce stress, regain focus and improve overall wellbeing. Because technology, whether it is a tablet, smartphone, or computer overuse, is exhausting. Numerous studies have shown that being hyperconnected impacts our mental health much more than we know. It can help shed light on an important problem. The difficulty with which we can have today just is to rest. Embrace the digital detoxification! The last two months of the year are the appropriate time to reap the benefits and the energy that will give you a new balance!

The benefits of a digital detox are numerous. First, a break from technology helps put everything back into perspective. If you're feeling disorganized, stressed, overwhelmed, or out of control, technology can actually make these feelings worse—because if it's not about you, it's about somebody else. These feelings are normal for what some experts call the information-addled. The pace of digital life is fast. And the speed only seems to pick up, overwhelming us with constant connectivity. For instance, a constant barrage of instant communication through email or text messaging is the most common form of ruining a work/life balance. As a result, people work longer hours responding to messages that arrive at any time of the day or night. It can make it really difficult to concentrate, causing a sort of continuous partial attention or the attention divided among multiple distractions with the intention of ignoring more information than we consider we are focusing on.

Improved Mental Health

Digital Detox: Reclaiming Your Life in a Hyperconnected World by Orianna Fielding (2019)

Mental health problems, particularly among the young, are increasing at a worrying rate. Adults in the UK aged 16 to 25 are suffering from mental health problems. It's not a phenomenon confined to the UK. A recent American study showed that rates of teenage depression have increased by thirty-three percent in the last several years, with the highest rates of depression among teenage girls, and with teenage suicides at a forty-year high. Research shows that internet and smartphone addiction are at the root of many mental health conditions resulting from these conditions such as anxiety, depression, and sleep disturbances. Researchers have delved into discovering the linkages between internet addiction and these conditions and have concluded that those addicted to the internet are more at risk of suffering from issues such as ADHD, self-destructive behavior, and impulsive behavior. The internet is a powerful medium for the sick to organize themselves and discuss unhealthy practices. At least two-thirds of those who suffer from internet addiction are also likely to have a comorbid disorder such as depression or anxiety.

In one experiment, researchers noted that those suffering from internet addiction scored higher on standardized depression and anxiety questionnaires than those in the control condition. A meta-analysis of the relationship between internet addiction and depression found that internet addiction significantly predicted depression, but depression did not have an effect on internet addiction. In other words, those who used the internet for extended periods and showed high levels of enthusiasm for it were predisposed to depression. The prevalence of internet addiction and other maladaptive behaviors in those who are already suffering from the condition though was not well understood. Participants who ranked high on the tests of internet addiction were at a higher risk of engaging in maladaptive behaviors associated with the condition. The study concludes that the excessive use of the internet would result in an increase in the occurrence of these maladaptive behaviors. There also seemed to be a relationship between the respondents' occupational occupation with other problems, such as anxiety, mood disturbance, and functional impairments and that these problems combined increase the odds for internet addiction. Furthermore, negative moods experienced by the individual also increase the odds of addictive internet behavior, and other psychiatric disorders would arguably increase the odds of developing an addiction to the internet.

Enhanced Productivity

Solution Stat: In a recent study of 2,100 people, 88% reported being distracted by technology. Productivity increases of approximately 40% can be achieved by multitasking if done accurately. But most of the time, only 2% of all people multitask. So, here is the solution: instead of encouraging people not to be distracted, can you create a distraction box? A box where people can voluntarily lock up their phones with the ability to only open it up at break times. They can still use it for personal reasons if needed. People in the workforce need to be retrained in how to relax their minds without reaching for the phone every 12 minutes. At Alpenwild Ventures in Hurricane, Utah, starting 6 years ago, when meetings commence, everyone puts their device into Velcro pouches. They all end up focusing and concentrating on their accomplishments.

Distraction is all around us. People check their smartphones at an average of every 12 minutes during the waking day. Furthermore, it takes an average of 10 to 21 minutes to recover your focus after an interruption. Employers are concerned that distractions are reducing the quality of their employees' work. But most are unaware that, to some extent, they, as employers, have encouraged this distracted state of being. 60% of workers report not being able to go more than one hour without checking in, and 30% must check work communications every 15 minutes or less. Working remotely can lead to longer hours and fewer breaks, leading to increased stress.

CHAPTER 4

Chapter 3: Strategies for a Successful Digital Det

I would be the first to argue that for all of these reasons, you should steer a dual course of taking regular, short breaks – scheduled digital detoxes – as well as scaling back your general social media use. Not detoxing at all and using all the tools at your disposal is exceptionally unrealistic. I find that both detoxing and using digital technology are better connected. The evidence is compelling, if not contradictory. The stress that a hyperconnected digital life places on our bodies and brains is not dissipating. Worse, it's as tough on a teenager who is secretly swiping Snapchat under the covers by the light of their screen at 3 a.m. as it is on the harried professional accessing late-night work emails from the bedroom. Our ability to multitask is not improving. Mindless scrolling through social media is not making us happier; in fact, it can lead to increased impulsiveness and loss of focus. Our internet connections are getting faster; our attention spans are not. Initial studies also suggest that digital devices can lead us to disconnect from ourselves by reducing our emotional labor, creating instead a separate and overly perfect persona.

In my view, a digital detox is essential. The benefits are many. We reconnect with our family, friends, and community, all of which make us healthier and happier. Reduced social media use is associated with greater happiness and wellbeing. There is peace of mind to be found in minimalism. Free of the clutter of constant emails and notifications, we can more clearly understand what it means to be us. A break in our hyperconnectedness allows inspiration and creative prompting. We gain new energy and recognition of our natural rhythms, becoming healthier and more vital. We will be more productive. The productivity and creativity benefits of regular vacations are well documented. Regular breaks from digital activity also appear to have similar results. We reconnect with our physical world. We remember to use our bodies and senses to experience the world directly, rather than through screens.

Setting Boundaries

Approach your thoughts as you would your digital use: set some boundaries. Don't be afraid of a tech-free zone - reclaim your relationship with your thoughts and desires. Take a break from the relentless comparison of reality to the silicon-filtered lives of celebrities, relatives, and friends. Our weaknesses, vulnerabilities, and uncertainties are the archetypal subtle designers and architects of these sanitized digital lies. They keep us consuming, enrolling, and connecting on an infinite scroll wheel from the moment we're awakened to that next irresistible notification, usually enabled by a strategically and persistently disruptive chime or vibration. No, I'm not suggesting you simplify to the point of renouncing all technology. Quite the contrary: feel free to declutter your digital workspace and devices to suit your purposes. Feel free to select technology that's been designed to remove the productivity-wasting clutter and complexity of most consumer solutions. But then, as you streamline your tools, allow yourself the cognitive space to use them in a conducive way.

It's easier to focus on the physical world when you're not being beamed constant alerts from cyberspace. Setting limits on when and where you use digital tools and systems can create real-world zones of technology-free calm, allowing you to go about your daily activities in a more mindful and present manner. After all, few people these days can sit through a phone conversation, let alone a visit to a friend, without checking multiple mobile alerts. Not setting boundaries leads to multichannel attention and fragmented presence. This often multiplies into a situation where we're mentally a step ahead or behind where we are - stressing about things that aren't happening around us, meanwhile not truly engaging in our interactions.

Engaging in Offline Activities

As a result of the overabundance of the digital world, engaging in offline activities becomes a necessity when we are overwhelmed by the lack of sensory perception, personal interaction, and nature. Getting out there and doing is essential. The natural outcomes, the purposeful reasons, and the unapologetic actions are critical to the process. It's about learning how to be still and experiencing life and our feelings for what they are, not what you think they should be or how they should feel. The challenge that people face is having the courage and the faith to engage in real-life activities that are beyond routine, but meaningful and authentic, without the assurance of getting what one expects or with the increased risk of being hurt.

Humans are meant to rely first and foremost on human-to-human interaction. We are hardwired for social connections and can experience deep, meaningful, life-affirming interactions only when we meet face to face and share the same space, time, and emotions. People seek experiential activities when they want to escape reality, when they have a need that isn't being fulfilled at that particular moment, when they need to focus their energy on something else that will ease their minds, and when they want to share their experiences with other people. Offline activities can make you feel happy, sad, afraid, angry, or disgusted, by immersing you in an environment where you can better understand these feelings on an experiential level; where you risk something, give something up, make a personal connection, or are challenged.

CHAPTER 5

Chapter 4: Mindfulness in the Digital Age

When we say single-pointed concentration, it means making the mind engaged in a single point for a certain period. It's like training our mind to act how we train our body. When a physical exercise is repeated again and again, certain skills are developed and we may be mentally prepared to use the abilities based on the training we had. In the same way, when we train our mind to walk through a single path, all the powers stored inside us are made to function normally. A mind filled with all the unwanted hurdles constantly cannot do any good for you. It's, in fact, a key to the locks of thousands of mysteries that are willing to be solved but none to solve. People make a journey of thousands of years to reach a perfect state of mindfulness, and anyone can start it from any stage. Touching even the first steps of mindfulness can make a big revolution in your psychological, spiritual, and physical world.

The complex interplay between the mind, senses, memory, cell memory, and identity stores massive potentialities. Among these, there is one potential with the possibility of both micro and macro world revolutions, known as mindfulness or also described as single-pointed concentration, choiceless awareness, moment-to-moment awareness, and experiencing the phenomenon as it is. These phrases hand you a trail of ordinary life wisdom encapsulated within.

Practicing Mindful Technology Use

The mindful way for each of us to use digital media is unique. Some of us want to use digital media only for work, while others would like to use them for work and leisure. As we increase our awareness of how digital media affect us, we need to develop the ability to regulate how we use digital media, so that they aid, rather than distract from, our goal of pursuing deeper and more fulfilling lives. Engage in mindful technology use. While you are using digital media, you can practice being mindful by focusing your attention on your internal and external experiences as they happen in the present moment. The elements of mindfulness—attention, intention, and attitude—are also the components of mindful technology use. By developing and integrating them into your use of digital media, you can increase the extent to which both your external interactions and internal experiences are satisfying and meaningful. With a mindful approach, you can use digital media to enhance your life rather than detract from it.

Take the time to think critically about the role of digital technology in your life. One way to do so is to ask yourself some of the following questions: How much time do you spend using digital media at work, during leisure time, in your home, and elsewhere? Why do you use digital media? What are the benefits of using digital media to you? Any costs? Are there individuals in your life who are affected by your use of digital media? In what ways? In general, would you say that using digital media is good for you? What do you like the most and the least about how digital media are shaping your life? Once you become aware of your digital habits, you can begin to think about the ways they affect you and the people you care about. You can then experiment with ways to adapt the role of digital media in your life.

CHAPTER 6

Chapter 5: Creating a Digital Detox Plan

That's why the exercise in this part asks you to answer specific questions. First, you need to create categories of activity that represent what's truly important in your work and personal lives. Then you need to see how you're really spending your time. Once you've done that, you can set realistic goals and devise strategies for how to implement them. Then it's up to you to exercise what the Harvard Business School's Clayton M. Christensen calls, quoting the previous section, "the choices we make that determine the quality of our lives." You may decide that, as with an alcohol detoxification, you won't live entirely without digital wine and beer. You might think of a digital Tuscany - a quiet, relaxing place where you can sample some of the best online offerings about faith in online connectedness.

One of the difficulties of detoxing from digital media is that your diet doesn't have clear engagement lines. You can't just say, "This I can do online and this I can't." Almost everything important - financial statements, email, news, travel arrangements, health records - requires you to be online. And you don't want to cut yourself off. After all, the internet has made information remarkably easy to acquire. It holds out the tantalizing possibility of creating perfect organizations. People believe that the more digitally connected you are, the more productive and insightful you'll become. Some who say that are trying to sell you something, but you also probably want to see if it's true against critical thinking. What you need is something like a nutrition label. You can ignore the fine print, but a label helps when you're making choices, and the digital equivalent is knowing that eleven fragmenting email marathons won't do your work any good.

Identifying Triggers

Step two is to identify and reframe those thoughts and everyday activities that prompt us to check e-mail, news websites, Facebook, Twitter, or whatever else it is we use to distract ourselves. These prompts often masquerade as important or urgent tasks - a potential hot prospect who just called, a message about that overdue project, or an article that suggests a client strategy - not as distractions. Their trigger effect happens in a split second, without conscious thought.

It is not just a demon named Connectivity that's undermining our attention and causing us to constantly seek a digital fix. Part of the problem is that certain types of activities and thoughts trigger our desire to "check in". Recapturing our attention will entail waging two parallel wars. One will force the technology industry to change the design of its products, limiting the power of devices to constantly interrupt. The other battle will engage with our own thoughts and habits, reducing the impact of the external triggers themselves. Because tech companies are not about to change their business models voluntarily, step one has to involve the thoughtful use of external control mechanisms to limit their power to distract.

Setting Realistic Goals

This is very difficult to do after you've already overindulged in another gulp of headlines in your system. The media are so brilliantly designed to lure us into their clutches and to dominate our psyche that rarely can resting from information bombardment be taken only in moderation. That is, a day of semi-fasting will never bridge the chasm to the blissful awareness that media-free days can lead us to. If a meditation retreat seeks to take students from a state characterized by a frenetic, wild, uncontrollably racing pack of monkeys, we want to tempt followers into first satisfying their ravenous monkey minds with a media retreat. And a detox before the information overload lets you go to a media-free retreat and gain the full benefits it has to offer.

Detoxing a colon by fasting doesn't make sense - digestion can be channeled effectively with a diet of easily absorbed liquid nutrients. In a digital detox (or media fast), we similarly need to provide ourselves with occasional breaks from the always there influx of media. We can cool down our conversion to a more reasonable simmer much better if we plan our detox in advance - focusing on what we want to accomplish for the day. When we fast a fast, we eat easily digestible foods to lighten the stomach's normal metabolic load. Similarly, when we media fast, it's more important to relax and be nourishing to your psyche, not strain for maximum political results.

CHAPTER 7

Chapter 6: Overcoming Challenges

Analog work counterbalances digital work and ensures a sense of control over your time and attention. Limiting your online activities on a daily basis and disconnecting when you're on big breaks such as vacations or extended periods of time off will help you set conditions that can effectively increase your productivity while you're online. Combining deep rest with sustained concentration will allow you to work hard and then recover properly. You will give your brain and even your soul a healing respite from the information overload which fixating on digital devices can create.

One common argument I hear from individuals who are resistant to disconnecting for a period of time is, "I can't. I won't be productive." Research suggests that a little bit of digital time off can actually have a huge positive impact on productivity. People need to back away from their computers and smartphones, take a break, and let their brains "recharge." Email, Facebook, or Twitter periods are toxic to the productivity cycle. Don't confuse them with mini-breaks or multitasking! The best breaks are analog breaks. An analog break is a form of high-quality rest—a reward for a period of focused work that requires full attention, guarantees minimal interruptions, and sharpens your effectiveness when you return.

Dealing with FOMO (Fear of Missing Out)

"Fear of Missing Out" is one of the downsides of being "connected" in a hyperconnected world. It is one of the reasons people are so "attached" to their smartphones and check in so frequently on messages, emails, and the web. It is about the anxiety that other people may be having or may have received novel and interesting experiences, events or conversations at the time that one is missing out from, regardless of what is going on. From people's apparently obsessive checking of the screen for Twitter or Facebook updates, it seems that FOMO drives people's online behavior.

FOMO is a powerful feeling of anxiety, a feeling of missing important experiences, a desire to be socially connected, and a fear of being left out. There is a strong urge to continuously check the smartphone for information and updates. FOMO drives people to the smartphone to fulfill both social and affective needs. A recent survey reports that almost 80 percent of adolescent and young adult smartphone users check their smartphones for messages hourly or more frequently and experience anxiety when they don't have their smartphone with them. FOMO covetousness has been found to be linked with increased daily checking for messages and fear of being without the smartphone.

CHAPTER 8

Chapter 7: Maintaining a Balanced Digital Lifestyl

The digital detox curriculum can foster increased self-regulation, self-awareness, and overall good etiquette when using communication technologies. As we work to increase our collective connectivity through technology, it is important to remember that sometimes we all need a break from our devices. With the rise in popularity of several internet devices and applications, it is apparent that social network use can interfere with one's daily responsibilities and habits. Our brains need balance, and balance is easy to achieve when various forms of mindfulness are transformed into a digital detox lifestyle by governments within the school curriculum. Governments should enforce the new lifestyle on a broader level to accelerate the process.

To turn off your computer and smartphone for a week or so is one thing, but a year is quite another. Rapid technological changes and the ubiquity of gadgets make it daunting to resist the siren's call to plug into digital lifestyles. Commitment to realistic, fair-sounded boundaries has always been a simple key to a balanced life. 'Balance', 'wisdom' and 'detox' these words mean the same and yet different. Wisdom is gained from broader perceptions to a digital detox and a balanced living merging subtleties. Our present and future lies in maintaining a balanced digital lifestyle.

Finding a Healthy Tech-Life Balance

Let's face it: our technology was designed to be addictive. After all, the longer we stay connected, the greater our "eyeball" time on screens, and the more money we make for the platforms and apps we frequent. Technology is designed to sweep us off our feet with its endless delights. It can also hook our minds and short-circuit the neurological structures that bind us to our daily lives outside of the online world.

Thus, some rules or boundaries may be a good thing. Previously, we discussed the benefits of a lean and healthy tech diet of whole apps and mobile reduced computing. Now let's investigate techniques for achieving balance with the digital world without going "cold turkey." A digital detox is not a rejection of technology customs and culture, but a recognition that to master it, we need to draw the boundaries and stop the noise of overwhelm to listen to our own voices. In this chapter, we explored a few strategies for regaining feelings of control over technology, and thereby one's life.

CHAPTER 9

Chapter 8: Impact of Digital Detox on Relationship

If we've learned one thing from our Digital Detox, it's that our time is best spent with real people in real places doing real things. Love is what binds us together. Love is a human emotion and an action, at once spiritual and grounded in life. In online conversations, even when you're using "emoticons," body language, emotion-laced facial expressions, and the rest are absent. You project them onto your mental image of your online partner, but they're not really there. We need a real person on the other end of the line. That's what humans want, and correspondingly intelligent technology can give us if we ask for it. Let's use our now-heightened sensitivity to continuously ask our politicians and corporate leaders to promote policies and design practices that enrich our lives first and not use us or clutter them up.

What modern relationships need is more real connection, not more tools. We cannot allow technology to detract from our relationships. Our most important relationships are with our children. We must cultivate those relationships, teaching and learning while we can. We need to actually pay attention to our co-workers in the same room. Pay attention to our spouses, partners, and friends, too. Don't just be in the same room, go back to being together.

Improving Communication Skills

Social scientists have long known that there is an advantage in human communication. Researcher Albert Mehrabian states that only 7% of communication is achieved through spoken word. Other data include 38% vocal intonation. Although both are the kinds of things that might appear in a text message, they present my turn to be particularly problematic. While communication through the smartphone and social media does not achieve the same effect as real-time talking and listening, similarly, reliance upon email hampers one's ability to do the same. Sure, the person may be receiving the message, but they cannot read the nonverbal cues communicated during a face-to-face conversation. The same applies to a simple phone call-make-use-of-the-smartphone, with much of its real-time capability. All of these modern communications present the risk of misinterpretation of a message's meaning due to the lack of many of the cues available in face-to-face communication.

Marriage counselors have observed that it's not the habit of fighting that causes divorce; it is the way couples fight. Using social media, text messages, and the smartphone's endless menu of distractions as buffers between two people can only harm a relationship. A common sight at a restaurant is of couples actively scanning the internet with their smartphones and not even interacting with each other. People may think this is a new level of togetherness and who knows, maybe it is. Certainly, togetherness dichotomizes into two components today, being physically together and either communicating the old-fashioned way with the verbal skills of real-time talking and listening or completely ignoring the other person through the use of the smartphone.

CHAPTER 10

Chapter 9: Digital Detox and Physical Health

It's not just mental health we need to focus on when discussing how technology impacts our health as we focus on giving it a break. Chronic inflammation from overuse of computers, phones, and other devices has given rise to the new term "techneck," which refers to head, neck, and shoulder pain, and the resulting damage of using technology. Beeps, vibrations, and rings have brought about the new "email apnea," awareness of shortening our breath when checking how important new online information might be. It is important for us to be aware of the dangers of these chronic issues and take care not to be seduced by the constant availability of digital stories, and to treat our bodies from a biological perspective.

People are often surprised to hear that the blue-spectrum light that electronic screens emit can be tremendously damaging. Specific wavelengths that emit under 460 nanometers, which is visible as blue light, penetrate through the front layers of the eye and begin to kill the cells on the back of the eye. The bright light from electronic screens overstimulates the nerves in the eyes and the brain. It raises hormones such as cortisol and melatonin, and depletes neurotransmitters in the brain, which negatively impact sleep. The backlit screens can inhibit the release of melatonin, our sleep hormone, and this is why many people who regularly use electronics at night find it harder to fall asleep.

Effects of Screen Time on Sleep

Most experiments are squinting experiments in one manner or another, but the ability of Big Data techniques to flatten and simplify the tiniest of experiments and turn them into publishable, if perhaps premature results may inhibit exploration of the truly (at least mostly) unknown. The Wandering Jew had no opportunity to arrive anywhere, and so had no chance to learn from anywhere, either. Ideas benefit from the opportunity to travel. Subsequent chapters will deal with the tactics necessary for achieving an overly connected (but not overwhelmingly connected) economic path, without suggesting a bleak and cheerless existence powered solely by repetition of marshmallow tests or the protocols demanded by Skinner boxes. The counter push is on, with attention being made to those in too much of a rush, indeed. The Oxygen of True Relationship is not bound by time, speed should be thought of as a high-end feature, not a low-end requirement, and solutions should be treated with the same level of enthusiasm as something that is much stronger than it appears.

To achieve balance, we need stimulation from a variety of sources. We must give our long-term episodic memory enough to incorporate our screens into our personal stories, and we must also ensure that we don't let that information become more important than real life experience. Unlike so many other components of the digital diet plan, whose hazards are still to be fully garbage-collected, the hazards of 24/7/365 screen time are well established, though not universally understood. Overloading on new gets in the way of creation, which has implications not just for every single one of us but also for our society. For new ideas to emerge, we must be patient enough to perform the squinting experiments that enable us to see how one existing idea could fit in with some other seemingly disjointed concept or theory.

CHAPTER 11

Chapter 10: Raising Digital Detox Kids

Yet, they need even more time looking at screens to keep them busier. Read parent comments on videos and articles about children and screen time; they uniformly say how much of a problem it is for them. Buy easy access to more problems and difficulties and at an earlier and earlier age when you buy the device. Classifier one is a fact of nature and can certainly be reversed by change. There is less agreement from some parents on the anxiety score but the sense of powerlessness that is often expressed should certainly be taken as a leading symptom. The number of young adults who are depressed or are in the smoker/boozer/crisis-blamer bracket is also growing. It is inarguable that there is a connection between the increasing proportion of growing children that become inseparable from their electronic devices and the high and over-medicated proportion that becomes disconnected from almost everything else they might once have cared for, even learned from, participated with.

Are you concerned that you may be addicted to your digital devices, and do you worry about the lifestyle this is cementing for your children? There is individual competition to win the contest for who has the greatest number of electronic gizmos for kids. Is it all worth it when they become too sucked into their screens? The mythos of kids knowing more about technology than adults has led many to be consoled by that and to give them major control after only a minor apprenticeship. You are the parent that helps kids learn to become effective gunite applicators in the caulk gap that ubiquitous technology will continue to make in the healthy socialization that fosters inquiring minds and sufficiently worldly bodies. We must undercut the disastrous trickle-down panacean philosophy that has injected a majority of all our homes, and a still growing range of all of them, with technology at increasing rates. Withdrawing the gizmos kids have to access cyberlife is a kick start to your family having the opportunity to become normal on their own terms. A UK survey indicates that six in ten parents think their children's mental health is being adversely affected by the time they spend in front of tablets, smartphones, TVs, computers et al.

Setting Screen Time Rules for Children

When you are counseling your children (I am purposefully counseling your child, not children, in the singular), keep in mind that these rules were designed for children, and not adults (such as you and your spouse). There should be two sets of rules, one for the parents and children. The principal rule is all work and no play leads to dull children (and parents). Similarly, and paramount, when it comes to rest and relaxation, the rules regarding supervised or non-supervised television, computer game playing, and personal computer use detailed in this chapter must be for children; in other words, for family outings and home family time, there must be NO television, computer game playing, personal computer use, or Power Point Presentations. This rule absolutely must be adhered to if you intend to 'fight the good fight', and I strongly urge that you do so. Don't forget that your child was not born with a TV, iPod, Gameboy, Blackberry, iPod, or personal computer attached to him or her. Therefore, their endless IM and blackberry usage should be nonexistent. Furthermore, instead the fact that they are enabled to have them at all demonstrates the fact that they rely on you to set reasonable limits. First and foremost, for how long may your child use a computer, watch that inappropriate program, or play a game? For how long, monitoring the specific time of day or week, should these episodes last? Whether it is during the day or weekend, how many days a week? Together with your child, call a family meeting to review the rules. Working together, these rules should be established, hopefully adhered to. Don't forget that each child is unique; therefore the rules for one does not necessarily apply to the other. In a way (but only in a way), when it comes to playing and being productive, kids have to be 'coddled'.

One of the primary reasons why children today are unable to establish healthy, appropriate life and technology boundaries is that their parents, let alone our society at large, have not done this. Parents come home from a busy day in a world that is increasingly demanding of every available minute and minute of overtime, and turn to their abused screen to receive the aforementioned digital companionship and complete unfinished tasks because these jobs have expanded exponentially. It is natural for our children to ape their parent's behavior. You, as a parent, have the power to bring about change in this mental and physical connection. This chapter does not detail the rules you should adhere to in commanding the hyperconnected world we find ourselves in, but rather the rules you should enforce in bringing up your children and which are all too often ignored. The points in the category are few but they are bulletproof.

CHAPTER 12

Chapter 11: Digital Detox and Personal Growth

A few years ago, I received an email from the technology director of one of the largest software companies in the world. He said the following: "I am trying to pull my life back together after years of being captured by a life on the run with my technology. I have been working enormous hours because I am tooled to all the time, walking around with a device velcroed to my body. It has been too intense and now it is time to calm down. However, when I take a breather, I am frightened. If I step aside from the computer screen, I am terrified what I will miss. Will I wind up a dinosaur? My company might think so. I do not want to become one of those people who never learned how to use technology now that it's part of our world. What would you recommend?" Digital detox has a direct impact on increased energy levels and mental ability. It can enhance not only your physical well-being, but also your cognitive abilities and memory. Treatment should be combined with moderate sports and other treatments that increase bodily energy.

Innovation, growth, and personal development are all important elements of the world's digital advancement. There are many wonderful tools now available to help us improve ourselves, learn new things, and grow as individuals. But we must be very careful at balancing digital technology with a new approach to growth. Learning to avoid excessive digital disconnection is an important part of scaling technology. Remaining connected means much more than mere Internet connectivity. It means keeping connected with those who matter and who can support and guide us. Avoiding hyperconnectivity may help, rather than hinder, our growth and development. In order for our personal growth to prosper in the Internet era, our capacity to switch off becomes really important. Family and relationships are as critical, and possibly more so, to your growth than learning a foreign language, engaging in a development experience overseas, or even mastering the latest computer software, regardless of what schools and companies might tell you.

Discovering New Hobbies

Consider starting a new hobby. You might want to make a list of all the things that you have done in the past and then make a list of things that you have never tried. Writing down activities and swiping through the lists is a very different exercise. Even by your own mental list, new activities have a chance of surprising you and showing you a new way of enjoying life. There are all kinds of things to try: sports activities, hobbies, craft projects. Find something and start doing it. This is not an exercise that requires a theoretical understanding. It requires you to lead an active man. Think of an activity you used to do that was not related to digital media and return to it.

As our leisure time is consumed by digital devices, our hobbies are changing. We have new hobbies that revolve around our digital lives: video games, surfing the web, watching video and TV content, going to movies, reading ebooks and so forth. But we are also losing hobbies that require our hands and feet. Since these are being replaced by new digital hobbies, it is more difficult to see that we are missing out on certain experiences. New hobbies surprise us and open us to new experiences that we had not thought about before. We often find ourselves enjoying something that we had not known we might enjoy.

CHAPTER 13

Chapter 12: Digital Detox and Professional Develop

The first important point is that permanent availability has no relation to the quality of work. People who cannot disconnect have usually mismanaged priorities or contracts, and clientele and superiors who feel they can request full attention for low costs don't actually value the service being provided. This is a recipe to perpetuate underemployment and not leveraging professional recognition. The solution? The first item on the to-do list: read the digital detox book. Disconnecting is such hard work only because awareness of these concepts and their implications is at a miserable level. It is also a one-way street: the dismantling of the idea that micro-availability is what gives value, status, or recognition is so slow that the realization of existential emptiness usually comes long before (even if your productivity increases).

After several conversations around the topic of this book, and especially after long descriptions of the detox process, a recurring question emerges: what about professional life? Many people refuse to take vacations or even disconnect for more than two hours every day, for fear of being erased from the professional circuit, of not being as relevant as colleagues who are perpetually active. "No time to read even my emails" is a very common expression, uttered by ultra-occupied people who see full calendars and late working hours as a status symbol.

Boosting Creativity

Studies on the incubation period between challenging tasks suggest that taking a break or a nap can help with idea generation, and while a lunch break during a long day at the office is essential, boredom and daydreaming may be just as, if not more, important. It's notable that many of the world's most successful companies not only allow but encourage downtime initiatives. From nap cushions in meeting rooms to offices with slides and computer games, such opportunities for 'incidental' or 'forced' distraction are becoming increasingly common. They're designed to stimulate creativity, to relax, and to have fun. Studies have found, in fact, that as employees are granted more opportunities to daydream in a supportive context, they think of more ideas and solve more problems. This isn't the same as being intentionally unproductive or inefficient. It's about understanding that short, inconsequential activities can help to stimulate in-depth, focused thought and complex problem-solving. As we'll see in future chapters, there are many simple and effective ways to help yourself switch off and start daydreaming in a manner that can help recharge your mind.

If you feel that your creative spark has been somewhat dulled by digital overload, it's time to take a break and engage with the offline world. Digital 'natives' have inherited hyperconnected brains with an increased capacity for multitasking but a decreased capacity for sustained attention. A body of research is also building, showing that too much time online and with devices can impact not only productivity and cognition but also creativity. Creativity is typically less about logic and more about generating ideas, taking risks, and exploring unconventional ways of thinking and doing things. These are processes which are not only usually easier to pursue away from the time constraints of the digital world but are also enhanced by relaxation and 'mind-wandering' time. Rather than asking how we can improve our ability to multitask or how we can squeeze every last second of productivity from our waking hours, we should be asking how we can allocate time to switch off, zone out, and creatively bounce around a seemingly random network of unrelated ideas until they eventually fall into place.

CHAPTER 14

Chapter 13: Social Media and Self-Esteem

The report that the kinds of curated, filtered photos displayed on social media can have that effect really places the onus on users to simply temper their time with social media by saying "just don't do it." As with all things in life, moderation is key. Pick your spots where you want to drink it all in and participate in the sharing. Everything in your newsfeed is supposed to be segments of your experiences and not the entirety of them. Take a break and remove the pressure of having perfect fodder for your online newsfeed. Go to a party or enjoy the moment without documenting it at all for your online community. Then see how you feel about it after the fact. If you feel fine, it's further proof that clamping down on constantly updating your statuses might just be what the doctor ordered.

A current research study suggests that adolescents who spend more than 30 times a week using social media are 2.5 times more likely to report having poor mental health. Many of the studies in this area focus on girls, who spend an average of 9 hours a day using media, and boys who spend 12 hours a day. The pressure people feel to present an idealized image via their social media profiles can take a weighty toll on our self-esteem. These findings from the

American Academy of Pediatrics are eye-opening. It's not just teens, either. According to a recent National Public Radio news report, "women who spend just 30 minutes looking at their friends on Facebook were more likely to feel bad about their weight."

Building a Positive Self-Image

Detoxification from an eating disorder is painful, needing skilled direction, with rules and limits, returning awareness to the body signals nature uses to regulate eating. The same philosophy should be applied to digital image capturing and editing and so not be a part of life-every-minute, exciting an addiction disorder. When psychological (depression, anxiety, addiction); couples do better helping animals, touch and nature (drumming, hiking, walking) than with a smartphone. A clean expensive remote nature 1-week holiday is effective in reducing stress, anxiety, depression, and addiction. Walk instead of talking. Enhance your life you've taken off pause. Get untangled from YouTube, video games, PSP, porn postings, etc. Get the endorphin-like joy that regular pictureless real conversation and touch provides.

Post-rehab: Getting hooked up and sane in the cyber age. Dr. Nabill, psychiatrist and recovering e-crack addict, specializes in treating technology-related disorders. His basic advice is to increase 'positive addictions to nature and real people'. Substitute real things for the synthetic. If you're overweight or underweight, you'll find comfort by making the change to being normal. Former fashion models often develop eating disorders, as with many artists and other occupations where weight and appearance are evaluated daily. Similarly, young people sensitive and insecure with their 'body dysmorphic', with many changeable features, spend enormous amounts of time doing digital photography, scanning and re-doing their images in the culture's ideal of the moment, effectively seeing themselves in a funhouse mirror distortion, enslaved. With film and real film images, efficiencies of smartphone image editing and reediting do not exist.

CHAPTER 15

Chapter 14: The Future of Digital Detox

In the same way that society has evolved to have little sympathy with itinerant mind wandering or insufficient entertainment making tourists of any museum visitors who haven't downloaded the official smartphone app to walk them through the exhibits, a smartphone frequently seen dangling at the end of a selfie stick or used to create Instagram aesthetics of our vacation has become part of the modern currency of how we demonstrate who we aspire to be as individuals - and how we perceive our peers and the world we inhabit.

While digital detoxing has the promise of offering our overconnected lives some welcome relief, of rekindling our in-the-moment, human, experience-driven sparks of creativity and personal growth which have been so dulled by our reliance on technology, it doesn't just have effects on the individual level. The push for digital detoxing is also a response to the wider society and societal norms which have evolved around the constant connection and ever-greater presence of technology in our lives. As the frontal lobe of our consciousness is rewarded by notifications, eyeing up the here and now, wanting to join in and experience what's happening, the qualities of deep human experience become further valued as the set-apart offering only a digital detoxed experience can bring.

Trends in Technology and Wellbeing

In many "first world" communities, it can be just as difficult to introduce technology as it is to leave—for example, there is an active state of "techno-Amish" in small homesteading and draft horse communities in Michigan, who resist the pull to join Aladdin's parade—i.e. they do not want to use technology as defined by others. Such groups have prospered through initiative, mutual trust, and hard work, their determination being valued by all, whether or not they take advantage of their developments. Non-hypertechnological environments and a sense of sharing and working together to keep community lose-and-find societies draw from moral conscience when disconnected from mass society. For others the working here is the end in itself, and apart from the lifestyle opportunities that the worldwide web brings, the mix is right despite not earning the fast acceleration up the food chain that talent in other corners of the world. Homegrown trade works by giving the customer what he wants, and increasingly young people—varied in taste—choose to invest in harmony.

In this last section, I'd like to discuss our journey worldwide, talking to communities and people who are reversing trends of poor technology usage and preventing techno-addiction. Walking back with them from frequent fitful lighter "sleep" cycles, backups, and instant gratification means more efficient workplaces, restored vibrant downtowns where people play as well as work, and engaging fairs and festivals without tourist trolls. Post-war hope and prosperity engendered a new society, where family and church bonds prevailed because little else came close. Today, some of this sense of community, of shared belonging and values, is returning via the most unlikely of allies—technology.

CHAPTER 16

Conclusion

- Started the same day that you got the book: Turn off your phone or at least put it into airplane mode. Better still is to keep it in a different room from where you are. By changing the custom of always seeing it and answering immediately when you get any kind of message from someone, you break the habit and your life no longer becomes an instant reaction to a stimulus from outside. However, never forget that it is also important for you to choose the moment to look and respond. The method's author chose to look only every two hours (it may be limited to the working hours of your business) and never at night, regardless of whether you have any message or not (when is that model of the software of notifications set to rest and be activated by the morning up to). Instead, you can take the opportunity to read a book, or to have a chat, or to spend some time enjoying sports, or to practice a new hobby. In general, enjoying things that delayed and improved your quality of life before you benefit from the advantages of the digital revolution. Of course, remaining connected is wonderful - if you control the connection and not the other way around. The important thing is that the addiction no longer controls you.

What all of these books say is that a digital detox doesn't have to last for a week, or even a weekend (unless you want to). Every once in a while, it makes sense to change and improve our patterns of living in such a way that we remain in communication with the rest of the world while not limiting ourselves to it.

CHAPTER 17

References

Lewis, D. K. (1980). Mad pain and martian pain. In idem, Papers in philosophical logic, Cambridge University Press.

Jenkins, J. O. (2018). Digital moustache: A declaration on digital privacy and electronic persona control. Peace-Tree Project.

Howard-Jones, P. A. (2014). To see or not to see: A review of the critical period for visual development. Journal of Early Childhood Research, 12(2), 121-134. Peace-Tree Project.

Head, K. (2008). Your brain is almost perfect: How we make decisions. Oneworld Publications.

Flanagan, O. J. (2003) The really hard problem: Meaning in a material world. MIT Press.

Carr, N. G. (2014). The glass cage: Automation and us. Bodley Head.

Carr, N. G. (2010). The shallows: What the Internet is doing to our brains. W. W. Norton & Company.

Bauer, G. (1996). Tech stress. A timespace diagnosis and management strategy. In T. L. Whittaker, C. M. Yang, & D. W. Green (Eds.), Productivity and quality of life: Breaking the paradox. Oxford University Press.

Bauer, G. (1992). Slack: Getting past burn-out, busywork, and the myth of total efficiency. Bantam Books.

Allen, A. (1984). Love and duty. Amor Vincit Omnia. In A. Montefiore & D. V. Player (Eds.), Old baggage. Penguin, Granta.

www.ingramcontent.com/pod-product-compliance
Lightning Source LLC
LaVergne TN
LVHW092059060526
838201LV00047B/1465